You Matter

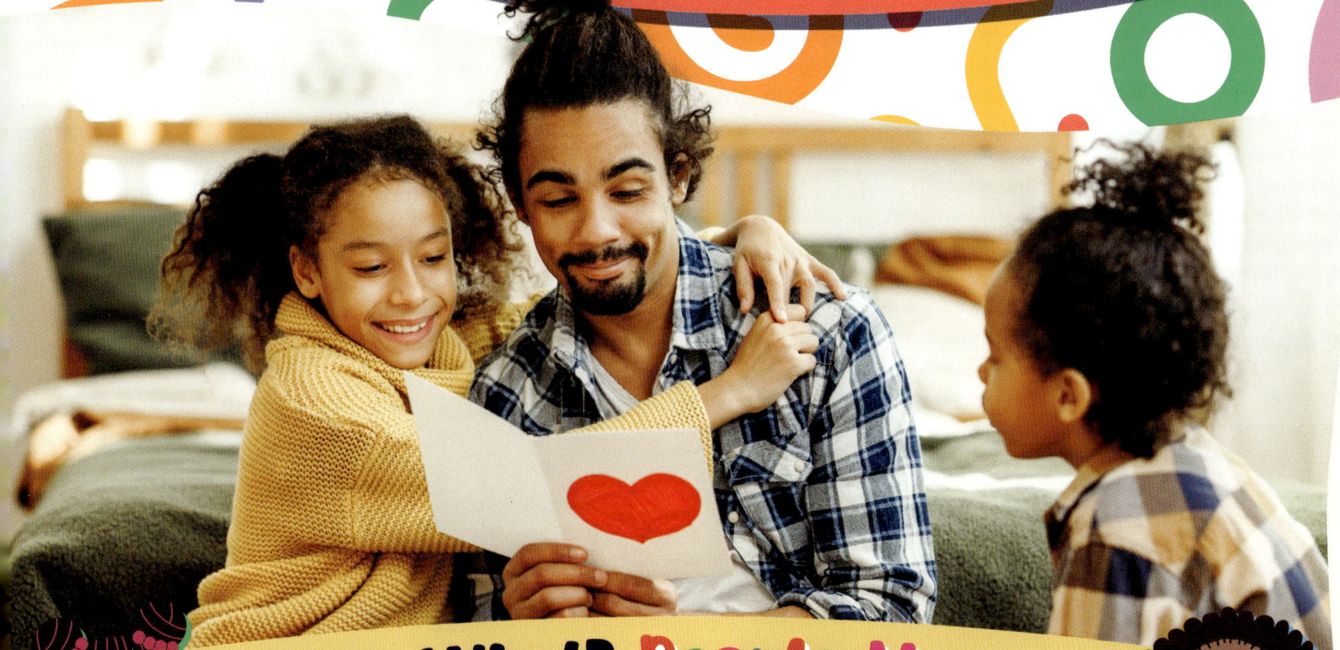

Guess What? People Matter!

Written by Charis Mather

Published in 2026 by
KidHaven Publishing, an Imprint of
Greenhaven Publishing, LLC
2544 Clinton St., Buffalo, NY 14224

Written by: Charis Mather
Edited by: Noah Leatherland
Designed by: Amelia Harris

All facts, statistics, web addresses, and URLs in this book were verified as valid and accurate at time of writing. No responsibility for any changes to external websites or references can be accepted by either the author or publisher.

Cataloging-in-Publication Data
Names: Mather, Charis.
Title: You matter / Charis Mather.
Description: Bufalo, New York : Kidhaven Publishing, 2026. | Series: Guess What? People Matter | Includes glossary and index
Identifiers: ISBN 9781534550339 (pbk) | ISBN 9781534550346 (library bound) | ISBN 9781534550353 (ebook)
Subjects: LCSH: Emotions—Juvenile Literature | Self-confidence—Juvenile Literature | Thought and thinking –Juvenile Literature
Classification: LCC BF723.E6 M38 2026 | DDC 152.4--dc25

Manufactured in the United States of America

CPSIA compliance information: Batch #CSKH26
For further information contact Greenhaven Publishing LLC at 1-844-317-7404.

Please visit our website, www.greenhavenpublishing.com.
For a free color catalog of all our high-quality books, call toll free 1-844-317-7404 or fax 1-844-317-7405.

Find us on

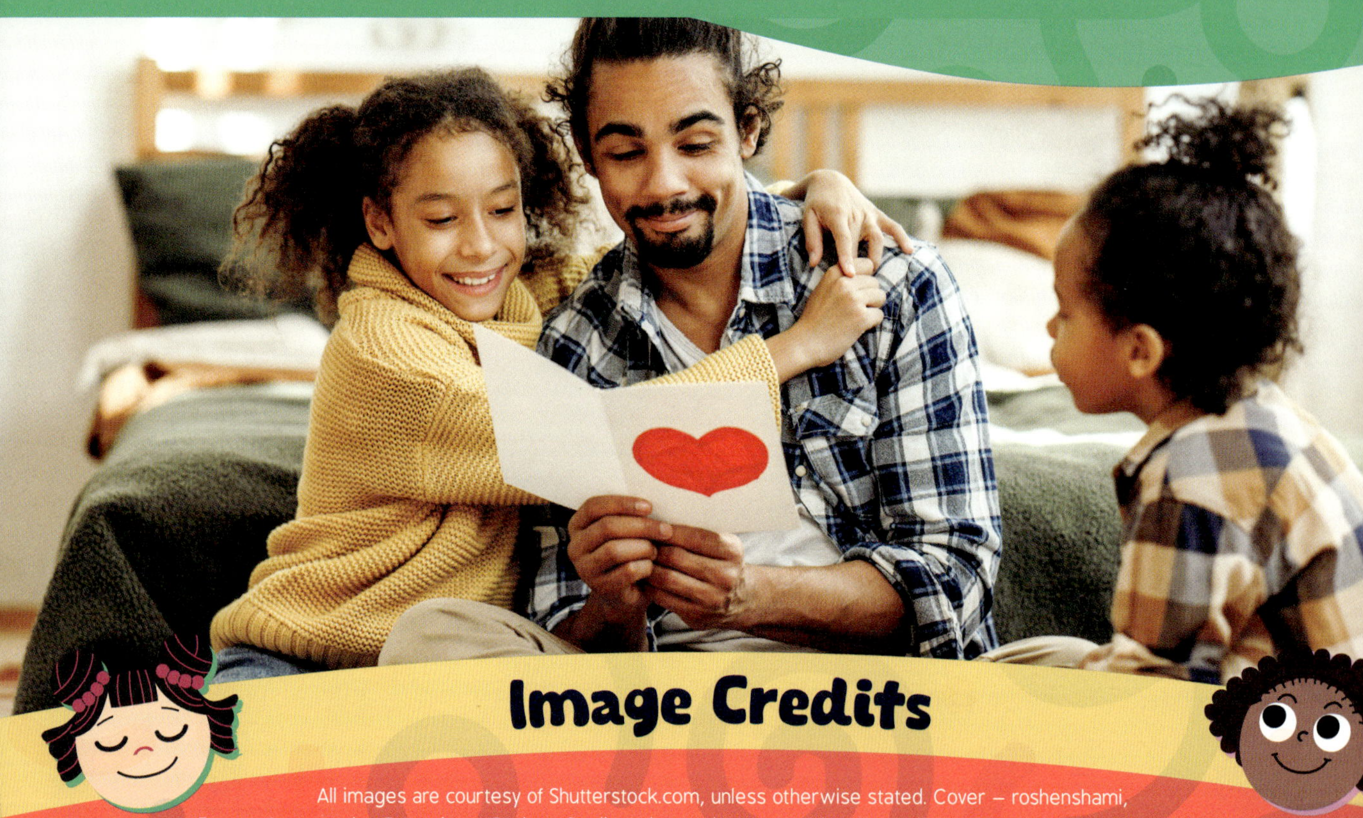

Image Credits

All images are courtesy of Shutterstock.com, unless otherwise stated. Cover – roshenshami, Evgeny Atamanenko. Recurring – Dedraw Studio, Lubo Ivanko, toranosuke. 4–5 – Thomas La Mela, Roman Samborskyi, carlesmiro. 6–7 – SeventyFour, Vasya Kobelev, BIGANDT.COM. 8–9 – Dean Drobot, Roquillo Tebar, Krakenimages.com, Q88, Roman Samborskyi. 10–11 – wavebreakmedia, Oleksandr Poliashenko, Oriol Roca fotografia. 12–13 – Ground Picture, Andrii Medvednikov. 14–15 – fizkes. 16–17 – Vasya Kobelev, T.Photo, szefei. 18–19 – Pete Pahham, Sklo Studio. 20–21 – Sergey Novikov, Alexander_Safonov, StockImageFactory.com, Krakenimages.com. 22–23 – Studio Romantic, New Africa.

Contents

Words that look like **this** can be found in the glossary on page 24.

Guess What?

Our world is home to billions of people—and guess what? Every single person matters.

No one is exactly the same as anyone else. That means everyone is <u>unique</u>.

Even though everyone is different, all people are equally important.
You are one of those people.
Yes, you!

You Matter!

Look at yourself in a mirror. There is more to you than what you can see. The thoughts and feelings inside you are just as important as the parts of you on the outside.

Your thoughts and feelings are unique. They affect your words and actions.

Being you is wonderful. But sometimes, it can also be confusing...

Know Your Emotions

Everyone has emotions. Emotions can sometimes be big. Sometimes, big feelings make us act in ways we normally would not. We can show emotions with our faces, our bodies, and the way we speak.

Sadness

Anger

Understanding what causes your emotions is a big part of learning to manage them. Your feelings matter, but it is important to treat others like their feelings matter too!

Dealing with Feelings

Emotions can be tricky to deal with, but they are an important part of who we are. Instead of hiding our feelings or ignoring them, we should try to manage our thoughts and actions.

Your feelings and actions can affect how other people feel.

Listening to music, taking deep breaths, and talking with people are good ways to manage strong emotions. Thinking about your situation from someone else's perspective is often helpful too.

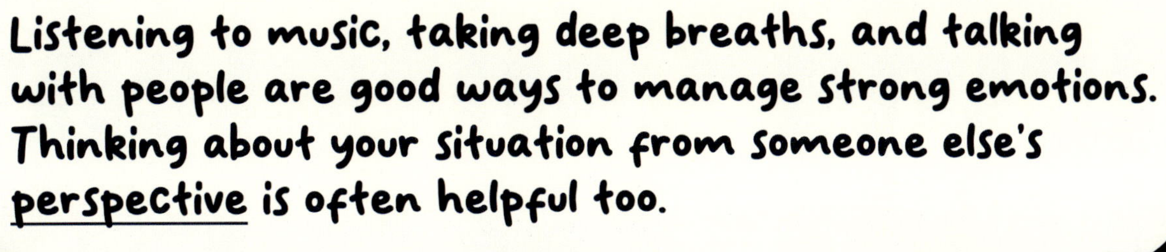

Calming activities help you take time to think before you act.

Being Confident

Everyone matters, but sometimes people do not feel that way about themselves. This can make people feel like they cannot do some things. It can make them worry about what others think of them.

Having a positive attitude about your own abilities and worth is called self-confidence. A healthy amount of self-confidence is when you see yourself as just as valuable as everyone else, not more or less valuable.

Believing you can do something can actually help you do it!

Challenging Yourself

Part of being self-confident is knowing that it is OK to make mistakes, get things wrong, or lose. In fact, making mistakes is normal. The important thing is to always try your best.

Being willing to apologize when you need to is important.

Challenge yourself to do things that are difficult. Make goals for the future. Even if you fail, there is always something you can learn from that.

What goals could you make for yourself?

What Do You Value?

People have different beliefs and values. Values are the things that are important to you. There are values for the things you say, do, think, and feel.

Honesty
Forgiveness
Encouragement
Politeness

Kindness
Bravery
Gentleness
Tidiness
Helpfulness
Self-control

Fairness
Positivity
Patience
Curiosity
Making goals
Creativity
Confidence
Calmness
Joy
Determination
Thankfulness
Which of these values are most important to you?

Strengths to Shout About and Weaknesses to Work On

We all have different things that we are great at. These are our strengths.

We also have different things that we could get better at. These are our weaknesses.

Strengths
I am truthful and confident. I stand up for myself and others.
Weaknesses
I sometimes find it hard to say things in a polite way. I struggle to stay calm when people disagree with me.
What are your strengths? What are your weaknesses?

Healthy Habits

When it comes to becoming the best person you can be, it helps to get into some healthy habits. You can practice different habits at school, at home, and in your community.

Habits are things that people do often.

In Your School

Have a positive attitude about learning and the future.

In Your Community

Get involved in fun activities with other people. Try to make a difference in things that are important to you.

In Your Home

Look after your health. Eat, get plenty of sleep, keep your body clean, and move your body often.

People Matter!

People have their own unique emotions, ideas, values, and personalities. That is true for everyone you know—your friends, teachers, parents, siblings, classmates, and you!

How you think about and treat yourself is important. You are important!
You are unique, you are wonderful, and you matter!

Glossary

apologize	to say sorry for something
community	a group of people who are connected by something
curiosity	the state of wanting to learn more
determination	not willing to give up easily
perspective	point of view
unique	totally different from anyone or anything else
valuable	worth a lot
values	character traits and beliefs that show what matters to a person

Index